FLASH FICTION

2025

COMPETITION WINNERS

500
FLASH FICTION

Dickson House

Table of Contents:
Longlisted Winners Farnahm Flash Fiction 2025

Competition Results 2025

Winners:

Main Competition Winner:
   The Song Of The Thieving Magpie by Elizabeth Meyer

Main Competition Runner Up:
   The Lighthouse Keeper by Trevor Flanagan

Farnham Competition Winner:
   Ghosts of Farnham Past by Anne Banks

Shortlist:

- Advice from an Urban Fox by Ruth Edwardson
- Full Circle by Dawn Cawley
- Gas Bill by Em Turner
- How Amelia's U3A Art Class Ended by Tony Oswick
- Passenger Injury by Chris Coll
- Pin Money by Lee Irving
- The Dream by Sheila Gove
- The Lighthouse Keeper by Trevor Flanagan
- The Song Of The Thieving Magpie by Elizabeth Meyer
- Wash My Sins Away by Ellen Evers

Advice from an Urban Fox

by Ruth Edwardson

I 've watched you turning up the soil in your territory, or sitting in your see-through den, spying on birds with your extra eyes. You've seen me too, if I've chosen to let you.

I like you. I've noted it's you who collects the rain for the birds. It's you who puts food for them high up in your trees, out of reach of those spoilt, well-fed cats. Did you know your male blasts cats with water and throws stones at them? I've noticed that your cubs like to play with you but they're frightened of him. I've seen him attack them: and you. I don't let my cubs anywhere near your male. They have a much better father.

Have you noticed movement under the cage over your peas? It's kept the pigeons out but a wren has found a tiny gap between the pegs low down. Now, poor thing, she doesn't know how to get out again. I've been watching her. She flies up but is pushed back by the taut barrier. She tries again and again, with weaker fluttering now. At the moment, she's flopped down, exhausted. She's trapped. Without help, she'll die. I see fear in her eyes, just like in yours. But you can set her free. I won't try to take her. I'll do us all a favour and go for those pigeons. They make better meals for me and my cubs.

Now, ears forward and listen up! Unlike you, the wren can't release herself. She looks completely spent. But just watch her. Given half a chance, see how high she will rise. I wouldn't stand a chance of catching her. And she won't look back. You're luckier than she is. You don't have to wait for someone else to raise your net. And your cubs will come with you. Cubs always follow their mother.

So what are you waiting for? Just saying.

By Hand and Eye and the Will of God

BY DAVID HIGHAM

T eak is plentiful here but hard. It takes a full morning to fell the tree with an iron axe that needs sharpening every 10 strikes. But when God made time, he made plenty of it, so the afternoon is for sleeping, while my sons strip the tree of its branches. Tomorrow my neighbour's oxen will haul the bole of the tree to the beach.

The following day I start to build my boat. Well, not my boat, a boat for me, my sons and their sons. This boat will let us catch fish for half a century before the salt and the shipworm and the barnacles return it to the sea as they did to my grandfather's boat.

I start work — I have an adze and an axe. No ruler, no iron, not even nails. I pick the natural curves and knuckles of the tree to craft the keel, knees and strakes. I shut my eyes to see the belly of the first fish she will catch for the shape of the hull will be the shape of the belly of the fish.

My sons help me — training their hand and eye as I did with my grandfather and father.

We toil through the Southeast Monsoon season when the west-bound swell rolls ashore from the Indian Ocean and no one can fish from this lee shore.

She is built. I walk round her appreciating the swollen belly of the hull that will be filled with silver-bellied fish. I smell the teak. I smell the tar. I see the prow parting the water and the roundness of the hull rolling in the swell. I see her list under the weight of hauling in full nets of fish.

I hold the hands of my sons and together we say,

'Protect us from the dangers of the sea, guide us safely to our port, and bless our efforts with abundant catch. Grant us patience and strength to face the challenges of the ocean and keep us always in your care. Ameen.

My ship is ready.

Full Circle

BY DAWN CAWLEY

Darkness, void, nothingness: Pale glimmer of light, pure fresh air. Brightness by day, silent moon by night. Shimmering stars. Sunshine and refreshing rain. Soft cool breezes. Sparkling water. Colourful plants and flowers. Nature. Chattering birds, complacent creatures. Humanity. Nourishment and growth. Abundance and delight. Awareness and understanding. Vision and harmony. Safety and security.Warmth, comfort, companionship and agreement. Reliability and help. Willingness. Pulling together achieving fulfilment. United.

Peace, pleasantness. Kindness and calm. Contentment, clemency. Joy and respect. Order.

Fair play. Spirituality, trust and belief. Sweet solitude, blessed companionship. Tranquility. Acceptance, forgiveness. Hand holding hand, reaching out, sharing.

Ambition. Hunger for power. Greed and unrest. Jealousy, revenge. Distress. Tension and trouble, bitterness and resentment. Hypocrisy. Diversity, defensivness, dissatisfaction. Disregard of others. Duplicity. Despair and weeping. Discord and devastation, self preservation. Disillusionment, drugs, deviousness, dread and abuse. Disruption, corruption, confusion. Drought and polution.

Sadness and shame, hurt and pain, not playing the game. Evil intentions. Alone yet surrounded. Chaos and gloom. Protests. Riots out of contol. Panic. Tragedy, terrifying and toxic. Torture and strife, cruelty and crime. Fighting and war. Wounds, bloodshed. Guns and knives threatening lives. Hands holding weapons. Fear. Bombing, fire. Death and destruction. Sinking. Fading.....fading.

Nothingness, void, darkness.

Blood in the Sand

by Andy Stevens

I consider my reflection as the train heads into the city. I have no memory of my middle years. There's no bridge from fit to decrepit, from straight to bent, just the hollow realisation I'm surplus to requirements. I'm a shrunken effete in an old greatcoat with a few desert campaign medals jangling as I shimmy along. Wisps of snowy hair cover a sunburnt, gnarled membrane beneath my jaunty regimental cap. My eyes moist and tireless are all that's left to suggest I was once something other than what I've become.

None of us could live with it, see. Least of all Alf who topped himself soon after we got demobbed. I'm here for Alf, for Norm, Stan and the others too. It falls to me to make amends for what happened in the desert. The day they surrendered to us, offering us the gold. That day of blinding heat, skin sores, biting flies and stupefying disquiet. The first shot was a mistake, the slip of someone's sweaty finger, but the devil's marionette took us then, and panic ensued. Many shots followed. A chaos of twisting bodies, blood flung from spinning torsos into the consuming sand. Then a terrible silence, broken by our retching and our tears.

Ordinarily, you might have gotten a medal for taking an enemy position, but we never told nobody. It's the war that done it, the war changed us. You can't know how the conditioning works, twisting wickedly inside you of. You think you can turn it off, but a frenzy took us with a craven beast controlling us. Six surrendering disclaimed Italian prisoners like young seminarians awaiting a miracle, their eyes wide with apprehension. When the beast left us, we were abandoned to our depravity and our shame.

I don't know why we took the gold; it was like acid. Once back home, black marketeers converted it into ready cash for houses and small businesses. We practically gave it away, just to get rid. All on the lives of those young Italians.

I tried to forget. Never told the wife nor our girls, but I couldn't escape it. Every bloody year we goes to the Cenotaph. Lutyens' brutal block insinuating, stark in its naked austerity and righteousness. Each year my insides tightening, burning with a confessional desire.

They won't search an old man, not one with campaign medals, shuffling along like a diseased vagrant. The greatcoat has pockets the size of satchels, plenty big enough for my old service revolver. I've tested it too.

As the last of our unit, it's my duty to lay the wreath. I'll gather myself together, I'll find just enough strength to take me up to Lutyens' whiter than white block. I'll do it for Alf, the others and those young Italians.

I'll stand to attention, submissive and contrite. I'll cry for absolution, press the gun to my temples and pull the trigger. Then I'll forget the day we went mad in the desert.

GALA

BY CIEL STYNES

A few minutes in the pool before the starting whistle, lining up to warm up, then it's all 'have you heard' chit-chatter-babbling beneath the surface, and I can't scream, not even underwater, then we're out all chilly-cold-shivering under coach's watchful gaze, a gauzy T-shirt to fling over a damp suit, but I still feel on display.

Skimpy costumed legs mottled white-red-and-bluish, all twiggy limbs and nimbleness, but I wasn't built for speed, not really, just for diet, and for discipline and for never deviating from the plan, but if coach says so then it must be okay.

Take your marks.

Starting posture now, toe curling round the lip of the block, one foot back ready to spring-kick forward, fingers steady on either side. I see coach's watchful gaze flicker, taking in another swimmer, younger, nimbler, just a little waif, really, but I keep my resolve, stay alert-hair-trigger for the beep like coach says.

And silence.

This is normally when my brain drains when I think only of the race and how it's going to be worth it when I get a medal and coach says I've got a special talent worth nurturing, but today I think of the little waif, and I think maybe it's not okay.

Beep.

I launch forward, racing start, streamlined in the water, no splash, just under into the silence, I can scream now, but why waste precious seconds, resurfacing, my legs a flutter behind me, ankles glued together kick-kicking to the front of the pack, two handed touch and away I go onto my back like coach taught me, and I'm scissor-kicking now, drawing away, and I know I'm going to win, and coach is going to beam big at me but I'm not sure that's the prize I thought it was.

GAS BILL

BY EM TURNER

D rip. Pause. Drip. Pause.

A droplet of water pokes its slippery head out of the tap, grows, then splats in the tea-stained stainless steel sink. Bill has been sitting in his cosy chair, watching the rhythmic sequence of events in his kitchen sink.

Life hadn't always been this dull. He'd led a colourful life, as verified by the framed *Commendation Award* on the stained wall above his bookcase, most covered by a brownish film. Next to it is the ghost of a picture that has long since given up the will to hang; the nicotine free rectangle testament to its previous existence. It once displayed a photo of PC William Brown, awarded for long service. The proud smile on his face is now wedged somewhere behind the dusty bookcase.

An air of neglect hangs heavy, clinging to every surface, coating it in a cloying yellowish film. Even old Bill is pale and devoid of colour, along with his flat, his clothes, but most of all his soul.

He nods off in his chair, wakes and glances at the clock. So much time ahead of him. The rhythmic ticking joins the music in the sink.

His joints feel stiff. He's wedged into his chair by his layers of clothing as heating is a long-forgotten luxury. Bill's breath stays in the air long after he's exhaled.

An unopened water bill lies on top of a pile. He wonders how much each drop of water from the leaky tap is costing.

Last week, his local library had advertised a 'warm welcome' for the community to enjoy the heat, have a cuppa and meet people. So, he'd trundled along in his best brown trousers, beige shirt and a tweed jacket to complement his earthy ensemble. The librarian hadn't looked up from the PC she was plugged into, and one other person was hidden behind a newspaper. After shuffling past the librarian and clearing his throat in front of the newspaper with legs, he did a 180 and trundled back home. He plonked himself back in his chair, certain his bum had left its imprint.

Drip. Tick.
Pause. Repeat.
He switches the TV on. The room fills with a riotous cacophony of people shouting,so he switches it off. Bill glances at the pile of unopened post, lottery ticket on top, then shuffles to the gas cooker by his sink. He turns the hob on, and the vibrant blue hues are dazzling. He pushes a corner of his gas bill into the glorious flame, and the post ignites in a blazing mix of yellows and oranges, brightening the room. When they become too hot, he drops them into the sink, until they crumble into brittle ash and fizzle out.

Bill turns the oven dials fully, but this time, not the ignition.
He pulls up a stool and sits in front of the oven.

He closes his eyes and drifts away to the rhythmic sounds of the drip, tick, drip, tick.....

How Amelia's U3A Art Class Ended

By Tony Oswick

It was no accident that Amelia's U3A Art Group met in the same hall as the Stone Agers.

As well as being a U3A stalwart, Amelia Baines was a long-time member of the Women's Institute, and so it had been no problem for her Art Group to use the W.I. Hall free of charge every other Thursday afternoon. And when the U3A Geology Group, the so-called Stone Agers, had been looking for somewhere to meet, Amelia's immediate reaction was to offer them the use of one of the ancillary rooms.

Although the Art Group members favoured landscapes, portraits and still life, Amelia always encouraged them to experiment with different artistic styles and mediums - although the W.I. Secretary had drawn the line when Amelia had wanted to hire a male model to be painted 'au naturel'.

The Stone Agers often spent their coffee breaks chatting to the Art Group members and it was during one of these that someone suggested, "How about painting a Stone Age picture?" To which another had said, "Yes, or portraits of ancient palaeolithic people."

To which Amelia had replied, "We've done lots of portraits before - but we've never painted pictures of actual stones. Now *that* would be a challenge."

So, at their following meeting, the Stone Agers brought in some of their finest geological specimens for the Art Group to paint.

"Be innovative, use your imagination," encouraged Amelia, "these are mere stepping stones to unleash your creativity."

Over the next few weeks, from seemingly innocuous old stones, the Art Group produced a collection of oil paintings which would have made Salvador Dali salivate. And, when they saw the finished masterpieces, the Stone Agers were overjoyed how their modest stones had been interpreted so inventively and with such originality by the Art Group.

Not so the W.I. Secretary, however.

When she saw the efforts of the Art Group, her disgust and revulsion was so intense that she convened an emergency meeting of the W.I. Committee to discuss *'these monstrosities, these atrocities, these abominations of human decency.'*

Amelia tried to explain that creativity was the lifeblood of artistic work. It was mere accident, she said, that the painting of a pock-marked boulder rolling down an incline resembled the features of an ageing pop star. It was never intended that the craggy stone with crenelated features, topped with a witch's hat, should bring to mind a politician. And in no way were the two curved stones placed together, with a Stars and Stripes flag lodged between them, a representation of over-sized American buttocks.

But it was too late. The story went viral on social media under the banner *'The Rocky Horror Picture Show'*, with the paintings boldly captioned *'Raggy Saggy Jagger'*, *'The Widdecombe Witch'* and *'Trump's Rump'*.

The W.I. Secretary and her Committee were even more outraged.

And it spelled the end for Amelia's U3A Art Class.

Oh My Days!

By Julian Cadman

Monday

Nobody likes me. The mornings are the worst. It feels like I'm the killjoy who's broken up the weekend... the first parent collecting their child from the kid's party... the person leaving the game ten minutes early *"to avoid the traffic."* The sensible one, that's me.

Tuesday

I often wonder if they notice me. I do it on a weekly basis. I'm your magnolia swatch that's discarded in the first selection round; the inherited bathroom suite you can't wait to get rid of; the chocolate everybody overlooks in the selection box. At best someone uses me to book in the annual servicing of, maybe a car or a gas boiler, but never something exciting like a dinner date. Would I be missed if I wasn't around — would the glory days appreciate the week wouldn't function without the likes of me? The quiet one.

Wednesday

Hey! It's me... the bridesmaid trying not to upstage the bride. Yeah, I know I'm not *"Saturday,"* but I'm the one that starts your week feeling interesting. You've got rid of the ugly sisters above, they're all behind you... from here on in the week's a ball. Market town squares fill up with visitors browsing mid-week market stalls, and football fans march in hope to their stadiums. I guess being known as *"mid-week"* you could call me the centre of attention.

Thursday

A while back I was *"The New Friday."* I thought it quite the compliment until I realised people just used me as an excuse to go out drinking and sober up in work's time the following day. Whereupon Friday takes centre stage, to rapturous applause, like I never existed. Taken for granted, that's me. Think Tuesday with bells and whistles.

Friday

TGIF! Yes.... I'm even given an acronym for being so special. And I've got a whole *"feeling"* associated with me. People knock off work early, stay up late — just to make the most of their time with me. I'm the tonic to Saturday's gin... a Wise to a Morecombe, if you will. I'm your new best friend... the fun one.

Saturday

Wednesday times Friday equals me — the one they all want to be! The hedonistic one. But I have my struggles too... like in those pocket diaries that give me and Sunday less than a stamps worth of space. Why does the so-called *"Monday to Friday working week"* deserve all the focus? Work-life balance could start with equality of diary space. Maybe cramming too much of the good stuff into one small period of time ain't healthy. Oh well, I'm out tonight so that's for another day.

Sunday

Save a prayer for me... it's been a long week. Days wise, technically unchanged at seven — as in deadly sins or, wonders of the world depending on how your week has been. Think of me as the one that bonds the end and start of the week together. The unsung hero.

Anyway, less about us... what day have you been this week?

Once There Was a River...

by Charles Kitching

S o, I sit beneath this old bridge, deep in undergrowth, the smell of summer waning, the quiddity and quiescence of the moment, in this still place where once there was a river...

As teenagers, reared in the post-industrial urban slums where there was nowhere to go and nothing to do, we would meet under a bridge where flyovers and railway lines cross-crossed above. We would sit with the dossers, the stoners and loners, drinking cheap booze, smoking weed, skateboarding in the bone-dry concrete channel where the city's river once ran, long desiccated by the city's thirst.

We were dreamers; mooching around with out-of-tune guitars and drums made from trash cans. It was raw then - the songs we wrote - under that bridge, where everyone met. I snogged my first girl there, sore lipped and cigarette-breathed. We were so young then, we felt there wasn't anything we could possibly do that wasn't right. Our wildest dreams weren't idealistic to us - not then - just destinies awaiting detonation. We were invincible, libertines of the most hedonistic generation, we believed. It all fermented there, under that brutalist bridge, all concrete and graffiti.

But what of now? Who still remains there in spirit? Most drifted off into the trappings of conventional lifestyles – a career, a mortgage, a pension, four weeks' annual family holiday. Some just disappeared. A few turned into the tramps we hung out with under that bridge; some dying of addiction, some surviving through 12-step programmes and last chance redemptions.

Only I, who so believed I would teach the world to be free, *appear* to have made those dreams real. I gained the fame and the acclaim, the riches and the accolades; royalties pour in beyond any necessity. I gained everything…

…and yet! With it…nothing. Because what was true, what was 'real', what made us free, vibrant and happy, was under that bridge, where dreams were still dreams and we lived on our wits where shoestring ends never met. Yet we 'lived', full of hope and unconstrained.

So now I sit, again, beneath another bridge; a beautiful ancient bridge that spans a stream which flows no more. But here it is lush, verdant with nature. There are no down-and-outs here, only me. I own this land; the whole estate, an ostentatious mansion that houses pretentions more than people, and rarely me. I am forever on the road: another city, another stage, another audience packed stadium, another hotel; playing my role, with the trophy wives all divorced, financially spoilt but emotionally neglected children. Wasted years. I am, in truth, lonely not free; tied down by contracts, tour dates, the expectation of fans for new material I no longer have the inspiration to provide. Only here, beneath this bridge, can I be alone not lonesome; where I recall the bridge of my youth, of true comradery bound fast by having nothing but shared dreams; only here, with nature's beauty, where once there was a river…and a memory, where once there was 'me'.

Passenger Injury

by Chris Coll

We roared around the curve at Union Square, the familiar screech of metal echoing in the operator's cab. A figure appeared, pacing nervously. He darted towards the platform edge —a college age kid with striking blue eyes and a spiked brown Mohawk.

We locked eyes. Through trembling lips, he mouthed "I'm sorry" before disappearing into the darkness below.

"No!", I screamed, slamming the brake. Too late. A violent bump reverberated through the car as the steel beast devoured its victim. The train finally came to a stop a third of the way down the platform.

I sat there, heart pounding, as the sweat soaked through my work shirt. I could hear people screaming in the station but couldn't process what they were saying. I realized that I was still holding my breath and exhaled. After a few more seconds, I collected myself enough to press the talk button on the radio.

"6-234 to Central. 12.9 on Northbound 6 track at Union Square."

"Central to 6-234, confirm 12.9. Passenger Injury. Show PD and FD responding."

The MTA investigators eventually came and talked to me while the NYPD guided passengers out the back of the train. A couple hours later, I was told that I was cleared of any negligence. "Just some nut job using taxpayer dollars to solve his problem," one cop said.

I often wonder why the kid apologized, though. For the mess? The delays? Or did he know I'd I see those blue eyes every time I close mine.

Pin Money

by Lee Irving

'That's four-eighty,' says the Post Office clerk.

'Four-eighty? Gosh. Right,' says an old man with a stoop. 'Cash or card?'

'Sorry?'

'Are you paying by cash or by card?'

'Oh, I see. Well now... Better be by card, I think.'

'There you go. You can just tap.' There's a pause. 'No: on the screen here... Ah, it's asking for your pin number.'

'Oh.'

'So, you have to insert your card. No: the other way round. That's it. Then type in your number.' Another pause. 'Then press enter... The green button. That's it.' We all wait. 'It says that's the wrong number. Have another go.' The portly man in front of me sighs loudly. 'No: it's not accepting that either.'

'Try your date of birth,' says the woman next-in-line, her beige cloche hat making her look like a relic from the nineteen-twenties.

The old man turns round and looks at all of us and none of us with the eyes of someone who feels betrayed by the modern world. His next attempt also fails.

'It could be the year you were born,' says the tattooed youth standing third-in-line, a toddler fast asleep in the pushchair next to him.

He tries again with the same outcome.

'You could use a different card,' says the clerk.

'Oh, I don't think I have a different card,' says the old man.

I peer round the customers ahead of me, and watch while he stares into the folds of his wallet.

'I've had enough of this,' says the sighing man, marching to the front of the queue. 'How much is it?' he asks, barging the old man to one side.

'Four-eighty,' says the clerk.

He pulls out his wallet with a flourish and inserts his own card, saying, 'I'll get this.'

'Why thank you,' says the old man, still reeling a little. 'You must give me your address so I can reimburse you.'

'No need. My gift.'

'Well, that's really very kind of you. Thank you. Thank you.'

'Oh, it's my pleasure,' says the hero of the hour, sounding like it's anything but, and adding as an aside to the Jazz Age woman: 'We'd be waiting here all bloody day for the old fool otherwise.'

But as I watch the old man making his way towards the exit, he gradually loses his stoop, and his stuttering shuffle opens out into a more easy, loping stride.

By the time he reaches my place in the queue, his eyes are shining with mischief when he says, 'Now, let's see if the old fool can remember where he parked the Jag,' whereupon he skips out the door.

Ring Of Hope

by Julian Cadman

L et's talk about my 18th birthday list... just one simple request. Ford Capri Calypso 1.6 GL, two-tone, silver and red, limited edition. At what point in that not overly long list was a family crest bearing signet ring mentioned, Dad? Honestly... a family crest? We lived in a cul-de-sac not a castle. And our so-called family tree had the genealogical equivalent of Dutch elm disease.

I know you probably wanted an automated treat dispenser, and certainly a fetching collar with paw prints running round it wasn't on your list, but I had my reasons.

And I lived with the disappointment, and the rings' constant attempts to impale my finger on every available filing cabinet drawer, right up until I fell under new ownership. At which point I got another ring to take my mind off worrying about losing yours. Luckily the drive to the wedding church didn't pass our local *Ford* showroom; it wouldn't have only been the bride's mother sobbing at the service.

To you that collar was a bit of unnecessary body furniture, but to me it symbolised the bond between us. Wearing it signified we were off out on an adventure together, or maybe meeting someone, which is when I got to show our world how proud I was of you.

When I discovered you didn't get that ring off a market stall and have the local blacksmith brand it, the gratitude and feeling of appreciation set in. As did the spectre of teenage ungraciousness. The ring morphed into something symbolic. A daily reminder of everything I hold so dear, when I put it on in the morning, and everything I miss when I take it off at night.

I'll never forget the cold feeling of loss that evening you slipped your collar. The sensation of helplessness as you sought indepen-dence. And I learnt something else in that moment... there's never a shortage of helpers when a British bulldog goes rogue in a bar!

The ring has aged well. And with age comes experience, and with experience comes wisdom. And whilst my 18-year-old self lacked both, now, 18 years after your passing, I have the wisdom to appreciate the ring as both a reminder of all the great memories, and as a symbol of overcoming loss.

And overcoming loss is the next priority, having collected your ashes yesterday. I start by clicking your collar back together and hanging it back up over its peg in the kitchen. A virtuous circle of happy memories.

So, what has the signet ring of truth taught me?

A good dog sits and stays in your heart forever.

Memories of a great dad are for life.

A Ford Calypso 1.6GL isn't.

Still Famous

by Helen Rana

The devil kept his promise. I'm still famous thirty years after we shook on it.

We met at 3am by the bins behind a grubby pub. Karaoke night. I'd just wiped away the vomit– too much tequila – and was teetering out of the alleyway. 'Suze? Tam?'

He approached. 'Lost your friends?'

I nodded blearily, annoyed they always ditched me for sozzled guys in sleazy places. He was not local. Unlike us, he was smart, toned, groomed. I tried to focus. 'Who are you?'

He shored me up as I wobbled lopsidedly. He smelt sweet, his tailored suit soft, his muscles hard. 'I heard you singing in there earlier.'

'Did you?' I squinted into his face – sculpted facial hair, flinty red eyes.

'Yeah, you've got a great voice.'

'Thank you!'

'You could be a professional singer.' He licked his lips eagerly.

'That's what I'm always saying!' How right this stranger was. He knew me better than my own friends and family.

He squashed me back against the grimy brick wall, his breath fetid, his forked tongue rasping against my cheek as he spoke. 'I could make you famous right now if you put yourself in my hands.'

I was tempted, my mind foggy. 'Really?'

'Oh yeah. I've made loads of people famous.'

We shook on it – my sticky sweaty hand, his hairy hoary hoof.

He kept his promise. People still discuss me now – in books, articles, online. Theorising about who killed me that night.

Me, the famous Karaoke Murder Girl.

THE BATTLE OF BATTLE

BY STEVE SHEPPARD

'A lot's been wrote about the Battle aint it, but I can tell you, mate, most of it's 'orse piss. I were there weren't I, stood right next to the King, bein' as 'ow I were 'is flag bearer an' all. You wants the honest truth? We was knackered is all. You ever tried beatin' up a few thousand Norwegianese then marchin' the length of England to face thousands more Frenchies with only a few flagons of ale to keep you goin'? Not that drinkin' ale did our bowmen much good. May've affected their aim, know what I mean? O' course, the powers that be – well, the powers that **were** – never admitted as much, but then again, a two 'unnerd mile march in four days withaht a rest, you gotta 'ave summat to keep you goin'. An' all the frogs 'ad been doin' was sittin' on their derrieres in boats crossin' the channel. Anyway, they'd already made it six mile inland when we spotted them. They'd gone an' ransacked poor ol' 'Astings on the way through, otherwise they might've got 'alfway to London afore we caught up with 'em. What's that? Yeah, bit of a coincidence that, I grants you, the actual battle takin' place in Battle. They'll 'ave a laugh at that in a few 'unnerd years' time, I shouldn't wonder. They'll prob'ly just go an' call it the Battle of 'Astings anyway, if I knows them monks what writes everythin' dahn. Pardon? You're askin' about the arrer? In the eye, yeah? Thought you might. Load o' codswallop, mate. Just the Frenchies biggin' theirselves up. It was puttin' it on that giant paintin' or whatever it were what done it. I bet they thought they was bein' clever. Just like they thought it were clever to invade withaht any warnin' while we was busy seein' off them Norwegianese in Lincolnshire. Sneaky, I calls it. No, see, what really 'appened were this. I'm 'Arry's bannerman, right? Big flaggy thing I 'ave to 'old all through the battle – bloomin' 'ard on the shoulders it is an' all - stuck on a long pole an' the pole's got a pointy end, know what I means? So, we're standin' up on an 'ill 'cos the king he likes to be seen by his men, yeah? Gives 'em confidence an' that. Worked a treat at Stamford Bridge. Less so 'ere though as it turns aht. I'm next to 'im, wishin' we was a bit lower down if I'm 'onest. Anyway, the froggies unleash this great mass of arrers and me, quick thinkin' like, moves me banner across to try and protect old 'Arold from the onslaught. Well, not the best idea I've ever 'ad, I admit. 'E looks in my direction an' sort o' ducks to avoid the arrers an' only goes an' pokes 'isself in the eye with the pointy

THE CHOICE

BY BRIAN O'BRIEN

P lease, can anyone help me? I'm trapped in a nightmare that started when I died.

I know that sounds strange, but I'll explain.

Years ago, crossing a street at night, I felt an almighty thump. Then I didn't feel. Anything. Nothing.

I got to my feet, or rather I got up, but my body didn't. I saw myself lying on the road, dead. A car had hit me. The drunk driver was sitting by the side of the road, getting sick.

Then, I understood something. I don't know where it came from. It drifted up in my thoughts and was there. Maybe it only comes up on death. I understood that if I chose to, I could let go of this world, float off to somewhere else and, well, I knew that letting go would be the normal thing to do.

But hang on, I thought, I'm only 21. There's still a lot of this world I've always wanted to see. I've never seen The Great Wall of China, or Niagara Falls, or Cape Town, or a million other places. I understood then that I had a choice. To go or to stay.

So, like an idiot I decided to stay and become a ghost. Not a scary one. Oh no, I'd be a tourist ghost, walking onto planes unseen and touring the world.

But that was then, and this is now. Now is 40 years later. I've long ago seen all the places that I wanted to see. I've been to every country and seen all the tourist sites on the planet. I've been to both poles, visited thousands of museums and galleries. I've toured the White House and watched dozens of movies being made in Hollywood. But now there's nothing else that I want to see.

I haven't spoken with anyone in 40 years. I've forgotten what a hug feels like. I haven't shaken a hand or had a kiss in decades. I've been a silent witness to joy and sadness. I've watched my family and friends grow old, sometimes die. I have screamed and cried, and no one has heard me. I admit it, I am very lonely.

After years of searching, I've found this spirit medium in New York. I'm making this appeal through her. It works while she's in a trance. Don't ask me how or why, I don't care, as long as it works.

Now, there may be other ghosts like me in the world, but I haven't seen them. I can't find a way to reverse my choice. I've tried and tried. I've yearned and prayed for this existence to end, but nothing happened.

So, please, can anyone tell me, how do you die when you're already dead?

The Dream

by Sheila Gove

'Alicia, wake up,' Mum says. Her voice comes from a long way away. 'It's all right, darling, you're safe now.'

She's interrupted my dream. Again.

The dream is always the same and I've had it a lot lately.

I'm fleeing down a hallway and it's terribly important that I get to its end so I can make my escape.

But the corridor is endless as it stretches in front of me. It's also exactly the same however far or fast I run. Plain, white walls interspersed with doors painted white making them almost indistinguishable one from the other. The doors are shut and locked and won't open. The floor has a white carpet. Bright lights shine from the low ceiling.

My heart races, palms clammy with sweat. Claustrophobia presses down on me so I'm hardly able to breathe.

How have I got here? Where am I? If I try hard enough, I think I remember a car, a huge bang and searing pain. But is that real or is the memory part of the dream too?

Sometimes I catch a glimpse of something in front of me. If I reach it, I'll be free.

Then Mum speaks in my ear, 'Wake up, dear. Please.' Which is most annoying as the hope of safety disappears.

'Open your eyes.'

What a strange thing for Dad to say because they are open, aren't they? Dad's voice sounds gruff with some emotion, when he's not an emotional person.

Lately there's been more urgency about them both.

'Please, Alicia, squeeze my hand,' Mum pleads. 'Blink your eyes.'

'Show us some sign,' Dad adds.

What are they talking about? Why do they want me to do such bizarre things? Nevertheless, I squeeze Mum's hand as hard as I can and blink several times.

No reaction from them. What's going on?

Then another voice: male, authoritarian. I've heard it before. At first it sounded hopeful, now it doesn't sound hopeful at all. 'I'm so sorry. Alicia is gone. There's no response. It would be better to let her go, peacefully and quietly.'

'No!' Mum's cry is heartbroken.

'The doctor is right, love,' Dad tells her. 'We're not doing Alicia any favours. Keeping her alive like this. It's been weeks now. It's not fair on her or on us. Let's allow them to switch off the machine.'

After a little while, Mum says, her voice very quiet, 'All right.'

'Thank you,' the doctor says. 'I'll make the arrangements. It won't be long. You can stay with her until then.'

Suddenly I know exactly what is happening.

'Mum!' I call out. 'Mummy, help! Dad! Don't leave me. I'm here.' They can't hear me.

The dream again. I'm running as hard as I can. The whiteness is blinding. I must reach the end of the hallway before it's too late.

But when I get there all I see is a blank, white wall. No door. No window. No way out.

Gradually Mum's sobs and my dream fade away into nothing.

The Lighthouse Keeper

by Trevor Flanagan

J ack was sitting in his spot by the café fireplace. The coals crackled and sparked as the children settled near his feet. Rocking back and forth, his easy-chair seemed to creak in orchestration with the fire. He watched as each child took a pound coin from their parents and placed them in the basket marked:

Tales from the Lighthouse: £1

All proceeds go towards the Seafarer's Charity

A hush settled around the group as Jack began. "Thank ye' all for ya' contributions." His gravelly voice echoed around the room. ' Now, what story would ye' like first?"

A clamour of voices from the children burst forth.

"Tell us one about the pixies."

"No, one about the kelpies."

"No," shouted a small girl from the back. "One about dragons." A murmur of agreement swept across the room like a tidal wave.

Jack grinned widely. He stroked his bushy, grey beard in thought. "One about dragons, ey?"

All the children nodded in agreement, leaning forward in anticipation.

With a twinkle in his eye, Jack began. "During the storm of 2019, I were keeping watch f' ships comin' too close to the bay. It were a terrible night. A storm unlike any before!"

He leaned forward, beckoning the children to lean in, too. Wide-eyed, they gladly obliged.

"It were near midnight when I 'eard a tremendous crash from above. Somethin' 'ad taken out the light, ya' see."

The children gasped.

"I rushed up the stairs and found the smallest dragon ya' ever did imagine. It were yay big." Jack held his hands six inches apart."

"No dragon's that small," scoffed a boy.

"It's true I tell ye'. It were 'urt bad. It'd hit the light full on ya' see. Took it clean out. Ships nearby couldn't see us. I were panicking. No ship would survive a crash against them rocks, ya' see."

"What did you do?" gasped a wide-eyed girl.

"Well, the light fittin' itself were broken. I 'ad to jury rig some kindling. But then I couldn't find a lighter!"

"So, what did you do then?" asked the girl.

"Well, blow me, though that little dragon were mighty 'urt, it dun leaned forward in me 'and 'n' lit it with a puff o' flame from its nostrils."

The children gasped, cheered, and clapped. "Where is it now? Did it survive?" one boy asked.

THE MISSING SYMBOL

BY JOHN GLANDER

I found there was a key missing. When I looked at the special characters menu, I couldn't find the symbol I needed there. I had a brand-new laptop which was supposed to be the latest thing, yet there was a character missing. I thought about going back to the shop and complaining but knowing the people there didn't have a clue about anything technical, I saw it as a measure of last resort. Calling the help line probably wouldn't help. The chances were I could spend hours on the phone being passed around between people and listening to terrible music. Going to the website wasn't much better since it took me a while to find the complaints box, but at least I had a connection. I was asked to state which model I was interested in, and then type in my problem.

There is no apostrophe key.

I had to write it in full, because there was no other way of shortening anything with the key missing.

The answer came back amazingly quickly.

We don't include it no more because its obsolete.

I wasn't accepting such a stupid statement, I had to respond.

No it is not. A misplaced apostrophe could easily start a war.

Again there was a quick reply.

Your problem not ours might be taking out all punctuation we don't need any

I could not believe what I saw! First the apostrophe, and then I suppose colons and semi-colons and ending with a full stop. All gone.

Finally I had no choice, I had to go back to the shop. I imagined a long tussle, but the assistant was almost cheery.

"Fifth one we've had back today. Reckon they've messed up. No problem, almost the same unit but with the key you need."

What I was being offered was fifty pounds more but finally I had the full set of punctuation.

On the news I heard a bill to abolish punctuation had been placed before parliament. I could hardly believe what I was hearing. Clearly the world was about to end.

THE SONG OF THE THIEVING MAGPIE

BY ELIZABETH MEYER

O ne for sorrow. I was unprepared for the first. Taking for granted something so natural, so ordinary, so easy to lose. Discovering just how precarious, how precious is happiness; is life. We walk on a knife edge, but never expect to fall. Contractions sharp, piercing my heart. Non-viable, they said. Common at this stage. You're young. You'll have more. Try again.

Two for joy. Twins, we were told at the 16-week scan. Double the trouble, double the love. Maybe you'll have one of each. I never found out; sedatives running through my veins, I floated formless, together with them for a while. When I returned to my body, theirs had disappeared without trace. Where had they put them? You don't get a grave at that age. We hadn't yet bought the cots. That was lucky, people said.

Three for a girl. Ruby, I called her. She made ruby red beads across the floor as I tried to clutch on to her. To keep her safe. By the time the ambulance arrived I knew it was too late. They wrapped her in a ruby red blanket and let me hold her this time.

Her tiny features were perfect. I didn't understand how I had let her go when I wanted her so much. My love was not enough.

Four for a boy. Zac nearly made it. I held him as he took his first and last breath, willing him on. There was something wrong with me, they finally said. My body couldn't hold onto them. My fault. I couldn't protect the ones I loved the most. I felt there must be a rottenness at my core, creeping from me, infiltrating the heart of me because my body was rejecting the purity of life itself.

Five for silver. Disappearing with each cycle. Each round of treatment another loan. Like silver raindrops trickling down the window, collecting, pooling, draining into the gutter. We can't carry on, he said. It's become an obsession, he said. It's not my fault, he said. He found a normal woman. And was proved right; she could hold onto those she loved. The fault was all mine. Not good enough to keep him. Not good enough to be a mother.

Six for gold. Her hair glistened golden in the sunshine. She was just a baby but played alone. They were more interested in their phones and friends and suntans, ignoring her. What was so much better about that woman? If I wasn't good enough, how was she? How did she get to earn the mother status that I craved? She didn't appreciate the gift she was given. It hurt to see her so careless with what I longed for the most.

Seven for a secret, never to be told. In the end something so difficult became so easy. Who did she belong to really? What gives somebody the right of ownership of another? Mummy, she called me for the first time today. I am a mother now.

Wash My Sins Away

BY ELLEN EVERS

T he thrum wakes me. I've been listening for him coming in but I must have dozed. I lie still, aware of the familiar whirr and thump my old washing machine makes.

I peer at the clock's green digits. 3 40. He's put the machine on in the middle of the night. My sleep deprived head is fuzzy but I know this isn't right. Bill is snoring, deaf, thank God, without his hearing aids. I sit up, straining my ears. The machine continues its cycle.

Shall I go down? What if he's drunk like the other night? I put that memory away. I swing my feet out of bed, sit up, heart hammering, reaching for his photo sitting in pride of place next to the bed. I wipe the face in the darkness as I know every feature of my little lad. The child we didn't think we'd have. Doesn't look like that now of course, my bald six-footer. Still my boy.

'He's not a baby Jean. Stop fussing,' says Bill at every opportunity. 'He's travelled the world for God's sake,' he rails with no pride at all. We don't know what he did on his travels and it's best we don't. But he's back now.

Bill hates him being home. They don't get on, never have. No football, no beers at the pub for those two. Bill keeps his mouth shut, wary of his son's temper.

I've spent my life like this, so it seems. The hours I spent with him as a baby; he'd never sleep without my cuddles. I don't think I slept at all when he was in his teenage years, listening for him coming in at all hours. And then he left us and I spent my years worrying from afar. Another cycle like the bloody washer now he's home.

The machine begins the manic screech of the spin, almost done. He's washing his clothes but that's my job. I push my fears to the back of my brain. Bill says I wait on him hand and foot and what's wrong with that? That's what a mum does. I like taking care of him.

The washer climaxes and softens into silence. There's a gentle bleep that indicates it's finished. The drum door is opened and I visualise the clothes pushed into the dryer above. Then a whoosh as the machine does its work.

There's a movement outside. I creep to the window, peer through parted curtains.

Outside sits a police car, lights flashing. Two officers get out, looking up at our window.

Oh God. Here we go again.

I wrap myself in my dressing gown and stumble out of the bedroom.

Tom has been in all night, I will swear. Washing clothes in the wee small hours is quite normal for old women who can't sleep. Nothing unusual about that. I must get downstairs before they ring the doorbell, must tell Tom to get to bed. I can do this. That's what mums are for.

FARNHAM COMPETITION

Don't Hang Up!

by John Kirkaldy

'Is that Debbie?'

'Yea, who's that?'

'I'm Sam, I stand next to you on the Waterloo train on the way to work some days. I usually wear a Man U scarf and a donkey Jacket. Can I ask you something?'

'Like what? What's going to win the 2.30 at Kempton? What is the meaning of life? Will Farnham come top of the football league? You are not that creep that gets on at Guilford that occasional pinches my bottom if train is crowded?'

'No, that's definitely not me. I don't do that kind of thing. Would you like to go for a coffee or a glass of wine some time?'

'You're a quick worker. How did you get my number? I don't go out with strange men. There are a lot of real creeps around.'

'Don't hang up! I saw your name when you opened your brief-case the other day and I see you most days at Farnham station, where, like me, you get on. I checked you on Facebook and I know slightly through work one of your Friends, Jessica.'

'So, you got in touch with her and got my number? You're a quick worker.'

'Yea, it wasn't easy. I had to go round to her house and do a lot of pleading. She took a lot of convincing. So, how about that coffee or wine?'

'No way. I have a large boyfriend, who has a very low sense of humour when it comes to strange men trying to chat me up. But Jessica warned me you were going to ring.'

'You mean she got in touch with you? I didn't expect that. She didn't say she was going to ring you.'

'Of course, she didn't. No woman is going to give out another woman's number just like that. You can't be too careful these days. So, I was expecting a call and was ready for you.'

'It's the only time that I have done anything like this. I'm rather shy, normally. I have only just moved to the area and don't know many people.'

'You might be in luck. Jessica reported that you're sort of cute in an awkward kind of way. You came across as rather desperate and not really weird. She has just broken up with her boyfriend.'

'So, what are you saying?'

'Get back in touch. You may have struck lucky. She likes football and guess what team she supports?'

'You're joking?'

'She's a confirmed Man U supporter; all her family are Reds for generations. She even has an away shirt and a scarf of her own! My advice is cut the coffee, wine or meal out routine. Next time, they are in London, take her to a home game and you may strike lucky.'

'Thanks for the advice. That's really nice of you, especially as I have just asked you out.'

'One last thing.'

'Yeah?'

'Long term, you may need to change carriages. She occasionally travels on that train.'

Ghosts of Farnham Past

by Anne Banks

'Farnham's changed darling, better than when you were little. There are so many young families. Little Finley and Eva would love the wooden fort they've built in Farnham Park.' I smile; I won't interrupt her 'big sell' yet. 'Gostrey Meadow even has a coffee van for the mums by the playground.' Her eyes widen with delight as she says this.

'Actually Mum,' I squeeze her hand, 'we've decided to move back. I've signed up with the estate agents already.'

And, as always, she was right. We moved back and I loved being home. But there was one thing I didn't foresee. Something that took me by surprise about coming home: the ghosts.

I see them everywhere. I see my teenage self, vintage flares bought in Camden, Marlboro Lights stuffed in the back pocket of my too tight jeans. By the river, in the sun, smoking away the day with friends. I push my pram past my younger self – she's a ghost; but she makes me smile.

I see the ghost of an ex-boyfriend. My heart beats faster as I'm drawn back in time. We kissed there, by the bridge. I walk past. I can smell his aftershave.

Sometimes the ghosts catch me off-guard. The funny, naughty memories are welcome, they bubble up in my mind and giggle their way out again. The dark ones hurt. They interrupt and stab their way into my consciousness. The bench Cassie and I sat on one summer's day to see how many sour apples we could stuff into our mouth in one go. Her screaming 'saliva injection!' as she drooled uncontrollably onto the ground. I laughed so hard I could hardly breathe.

It hurts to see that bench in Gostrey Meadow. I avoid it and walk the long way home, pushing my daughter up the hill as quickly as possible. I can't think about suicide straight after toddler group.

I tell mum about the ghosts. 'You need to make your peace with them, darling. Poor Cassie.' I look away, I don't like crying. 'I know it's difficult with her grave miles away...but maybe that bench is somewhere you could go to mourn her.' Her words grate and jar. She looks at me pointedly, 'Have you ever really mourned her?'

I go to Gostrey's alone one evening. I force myself to sit on it. I relive the sour apples; I drag up memories of her. My heart pulls back hard. It hurts like hell but this time I keep going, I push through. And so they come, the tears. They crash in on me. I whisper, 'I wish you hadn't, I miss you'. Something breaks in me that evening and mends all at the same time.

When I walk past now, her ghost is sitting next to mine. Stuck at 13 and laughing. I don't avoid the bench. I touch it gently. Sometimes I talk to her, 'I'll stop to say hello more often, promise.' Her ghost will always be there for me to visit.

May Day

BY ALAN FINDLAY

Jacqueline Potter was distraught. Year 8 were over-excited. One mention of Mayday and they were out of their seats, dancing round an imaginary maypole. That was bad enough, but they were supposed to be performing in front of the Mayor that afternoon.

'Children, please,' said Jacqueline. The rioting children took no notice; Sam gave Annabel a kiss and the rest of the class giggled.

Then she remembered the whistle. Her Polish partner Lech had given her a Polish police whistle to use on just such an occasion – heaven knew how he had come by it: probably best not to ask. She put it to her lips and blew.

The effect was instantaneous. The children froze, then, mouths agape, went to their tables. They sat still, as if caught by ash at Herculaneum. Jacqueline found and dropped a pin; the sound could be heard all round the room.

'Thank you, class,' said Jacqueline. 'Ben, is that a mobile phone? Give it to me. You can have it back at the end of the day.'

At the same time, in a marquee in Farnham Park, Pete Robinson was busy twiddling knobs and pushing buttons in the apparently vain hope of finding some music to accompany the children dancing round the maypole. He had a bit of a crush on Jacqueline and he wanted to make a good impression on her, but at the current rate of progress it seemed that that was likely to be another vain hope.

'I got Radio Beijing just now, so you would think I could find some English country dance music,' he moaned.

Jacqueline could wait no longer, and led the children out to the park. They stood in position, each holding one end of a ribbon, the other end of which was attached to the maypole in the centre of the area.

Suddenly the loudspeakers positioned in trees round the edge of the park burst into life, crackling and spluttering. Pete and two friends had spent most of the previous evening stringing the speakers up and they seemed to be working loud and clear. They were connected to his music centre and this was one piece of his system that worked – perhaps too well.

'Mayday, mayday. This is the yacht *Maypole Dancer.* We are on fire and sinking.' There followed the yacht's position coordinates.

'Quick, Ben here's your phone. You can dial 999 and then hand the phone back to me so that I can speak to the Coastguard.'

Ben assumed an air of self-importance as he dialled the number and then passed the phone back to Jacqueline who started talking urgently to the authorities. Luckily, she remembered the details given by the stricken yacht and was able to repeat them to the authorities.

Then the strains of 'An English Country Garden' poured forth from the loudspeakers. Left to their own devices, the children started to dance round the maypole. Within minutes, there was a monumental tangle, just as the Mayor arrived.

P.P.S.

BY TIM KIRTON

When the Pandemic restrictions kicked in, John James Buchanan was sixty years old. He became a stickler to the rules adhering almost religiously to the ever-changing governmental recommendations without hesitation.

He took his exercise in his back garden. He had his food delivered. His groceries were cleansed thoroughly with anti-bac wipes to prevent cross-contamination.

He avoided personal contact with anyone, quite literally 'Like the Plague'. When he remembered he even accompanied washing his hands with a full rendition of 'Happy Birthday'; just as Boris had instructed him to do.

Now a year and a half later Lockdown was over.

After waiting several weeks for his food stocks to diminish completely, he eventually emerged from his house like a butterfly abandoning its chrysalis. Free.

He'd taken the old familiar walk into town a thousand times before, but it somehow felt strange today. Alien.

He certainly wasn't prepared for what greeted him.

The world had changed.

He encountered an army of women who regardless of shape or size wore a uniform of skin-tight shorts that revealed most of the cheeks of their backsides. Their lips were 'plumped up'; 'Donald Duck' like. Below what looked like stick-on thick black 'Groucho Marx' eyebrows were it seemed to him, the borrowed eyelashes of camels. These 'lookalike ladies' all had a fluorescent orange hue. Fake tan had been applied liberally but patchily he supposed with something resembling a flannel.

The men wore long, unkempt, hairy beards. Their arms and legs had been covered in nondescript, heavily inked tattoos.

Huge plumes of sickly-scented vaporised smoke enveloped family groups as they walked the pavements. Incessant barking 'Something-A-Poos' and badly mannered children dictated the pace.

Cars had been replaced by 'Spaceships'; some of which in the supermarket carpark had been 'plugged in'; waiting for take-off.

He sought solace in the café and was eventually served a simple black coffee from a shoulder-shrugging Barista whose options concerning the different flavour combinations on offer had fallen on deaf ears.

He sat outside.

The conversations around him were loud and monosyllabic.

He never eavesdropped but was afforded no choice.

Everybody wanted to hear, needed to hear, to share.

He listened to the same new expressions over and over again;

"It is what it is", " Yes definitely;100 Percent", " Really!? That's Awesome!".

Apparently, 'Awesome!' could now be attributed to something as trivial as your offspring wiping their nose or using the toilet without any adult supervision.

When he was nine he had to catch a bus and then walk a mile to get to primary school. He didn't remember his parents ever telling him he was 'Awesome!'.

According to John 'Awesome!' should only be ascribed to events that were truly 'Awe' inspiring. Natural spectacles such as Halley's comet or a total solar eclipse. Watching a kestrel hover motionless above its quarry. Witnessing the sonic boom of Concorde.

Completely discombobulated by this new **P**ost **P**andemic **S**ociety, he numbly left the café and the metropolis and crawled back to the sanctuary of his cocoon.

Store Ghost

by Richard Fuller

L ucy stopped at the door marked *Staff Entrance*, stomach tingling. Her first job. Ok only temporary. She was home from Uni for Christmas and was standing outside Farnham's only department store, ready to help with the Yule-tide rush.

By mid-morning she'd been given the history of the shop-opened in 1881 as a drapery store by George Elphick, shown to her locker and introduced to her colleagues. Head spinning she was glad of the lunch break to have a sit down and chat with her new friend Judy, who had green hair, a bright red elf jumper, and twinkle in her eye.

Judy stopped mid sandwich and looked straight at Lucy.

'What?'

'OMG. No one told you, did they?'

'Told me what?'

'About the Ghost.

'They don't exist.' Lucy put her cup down with a grin. 'I bet you're winding me up.'

'No, pet. Ever since the family sold out the business in 2004, strange things have happened. It's like old George has come back seeking revenge.'

'Go on. What things?'

Well stuff, you know: things move, writing appears, cold chills. Seems he hates anything new and that includes staff...'

'Oh. Okay.' She dragged out the last word.

Lucy was a little less enthusiastic arriving for work the next day. What if the ghost really did exist? She stuffed her bag into her locker and gasped. Her work pass was hanging from the mirror on the back of the door. She was sure she'd left it on the shelf. But worse, written on the mirror in her lipstick were the words KEL CHIPS. Over lunch she told Judy.

'Ahh, I see you've met the ghost. Most of us have, early on.'

Next day, after checking it was still locked, she tentatively opened her locker. Different coloured lipstick but the words EG GORE were there on the mirror.

'Judy, what does it mean?'

'No idea love.'

'I mean the words. What are they talking about?'

Why not ask old Malcolm, he's been here years, he may know.

Malcolm smiled when Lucy asked him but merely shrugged. As the days passed Lucy dreaded starting work more and more. Her mum was asking questions and she daren't admit the reason. By now she'd had SPICK HEL, ROE GEG and HIS PLECK on the mirror.

Judy seemed to be enjoying Lucy's discomfort, which got her thinking. And then it hit her. Of course.

The next day Lucy was in very early and hid in the locker room. Waited for Judy to arrive and open her own locker. Watched Judy jump as she read the words SICK HELP on the mirror. Lucy stepped out.

'No need to worry, Judy, it's not a ghost, just someone writing anagrams of George or Elphicks.' With that Lucy turned to the laughing security guard who had also stepped out of hiding and was holding his master key up.

Farnham Flash Fiction Competition

The Farnham Flash Fiction Competition is a small, locally run contest where both local and international authors compete to craft compelling stories in 500 words or less.

Find out more: https://www.flashfiction500.com/

Printed in Dunstable, United Kingdom